SURVIVORS

To my dear friend...
I love you...
Stan

SURVIVORS

AN ANTHOLOGY OF WORK CREATED IN
THE WAKE OF HURRICANE MICHAEL

EDITED BY TONY SIMMONS

-JAY

DEDICATION

For those who continue to struggle, and for those who had to go.

ACKNOWLEDGMENTS

The Syndicate would like to acknowledge the motivational work of Jessica St. Hill, who started a Facebook page encouraging people to share the work they were making after the storm, and Jason Hedden, who posted daily (sometimes multiple posts) about his experiences, his art, and news of service to his followers.

SURVIVORS

UNTITLED
HEATHER CLEMENTS
(HeatherClementsArt.com)
~

Filled with so much guilt,
Looking at the ruins of
The house that was mine.

— *Jessica St. Hill*

~

DEAR MICHAEL
JASON HEDDEN

Can I call you Mike?
Turn down your wind a minute and listen to me
This is important

I know many Mikes
None like you
You confuse me

Why did you come here? What did you want? What are you trying
Never mind
I've figured it out

You've given me time to think in the dark
Thank you for that

I owe you an apology
You heard me right

I hated you
You've taken lives
You've stolen from so many

People I know
People I love

BUT

I'm not mad anymore
I want to thank you

Because of you
I spent a day with my precious niece in a car shade fort
She's so smart it's scary
Mornings are her favorite
Just like me
We made a bubble dance
She read me a book
She loves jingle bells

Why did I wait so long?

Because of you
I sat in the home of an artist I know
And she sat in mine
I call her friend but we were not close
I learned of her life and she learned of mine
She focused my thoughts through her way of seeing the world

I passed her words on to others
they've carried us through

Why did I wait so long?

Because of you
A father of a friend slept in my home
I've known this man for 24 years yet had never spoke
Not about things that matter
He made fun of my beer and we talked of his youth

Why did I wait so long?

Because of you
I prayed with a stranger at Wal-Mart near soap
It was awkward at first
My prayers so old I'd forgotten the words
But when she asked I couldn't say no
When I came to her aisle
She seemed too cheerful for one wearing a vest so blue

Her smile big and voice cheerful
Her eyes gave her away

I asked how she was and then the dam broke
She lost her home
We fumbled with new dumb phones slippery from tears
Hers and mine
She reminded me of my students
We now text to check in

Why did I wait so long?

Because of you
I see clearly through eyes washed with tears

Because of you
Strangers are neighbors
Neighbors are friends
Friends are family
Family is wealth

Because of you
Hugs are longer
Eyes meet and hold

I may hate you again as the loss lingers on
But for today
I see the gifts

Because of you

~

I duct taped my house
and my neighbor's blue Camry.
Thanks, Mike. You asshat.

— *Jason Hedden*

~

IN THE WHITE-OUT
DEBRA SIMMONS

~

Trees are uprooted
Squirrels clambering on my roof
Acorns anyone?

— *Donna Williams*

~

FROM A DISTANCE
RIVER JORDAN

I came into the world in the month of September. The great time of hurricanes. Saltwater runs through my veins. As one old man once told me, "Girl you're not local, you're plum local."

"Yes, sir," I said. "Pure native."

As I write these words, I'm looking over this hill from Tennessee—but I can see those waves crashing, hear the pounding of the Gulf, the slash and snap of the palms wild from the wind.

I've ridden out more tropical storms than I can remember. For about fifteen solid years I've made Tennessee my home, but it's in my blood to stock up on batteries, water, canned food. To hunker down and hope.

Hurricanes.

They've been second nature to me. The kind of native knowledge that would laugh at a Category Two as nothing more than a bad rain storm. One that would weather a Three without worry. Hunker down. Prepare. Stock up and stay down.

Every year, we had our little brick house turned into Noah's Ark full of cousins and animals and family. My mother managed a restaurant right on the beach where I worked every summer. People sat at tables by the water and watched the moonlight on the waves as they rolled up on the shore. Every year, we saw that the restaurant was bordered up and prayed for the best through the hurricanes. Every single year. A part of life.

In the Summer of '69, my mother and I drove through Mississippi from Panama City. My father was stationed at Ft. Polk, Louisiana, and we were on the road for a visit. It was just post-Camille, and the news had told us everything and nothing at all. There was no explanation for the truth our eyes revealed. The devastation in full color was stark, complete, unsettling.

We knew of course—everything. The television had been full of images and reports. A Category Five hurricane takes no prisoners, makes no deals. We hit Biloxi and fell silent. War ships had been tossed like toy boats. Chunks of the highway were missing. Homes destroyed. Trees broken and blown away. It was a graveyard for which we were ill-prepared. Television lies. The images are beyond reach and heartbeat. The brain processes it all from afar. The heart never skips a beat.

~

Hurricane Michael is bearing down. Has grown to be a Two, then a Three, and is now pushing Four. Cousin Deb calls me and says she has left her house on the beach and gone "in town." This is our safe card. Our sure bet. Cross Hathaway Bridge, get off the beach, away from the Gulf. Find friends, get in a brick house. Let the wolf blow, all will be well.

Experience can be a folly of a teacher. Time-tested and tricky. Michael rolls forward and is coming too fast, too hard. Something has shifted and we're not certain what it is, but it bodes not well at all. Darkness falls.

Cousin Deb says, "Hey, man, just letting you know I'm gonna save my battery now. I'm signing off."

I don't feel well. We've weathered most every hurricane of my life together. When she hangs up I feel disoriented. Lost. As if something just "ain't right." I flip on the television and watch, helpless from a distance. Night endures. By daylight, getting out has come and gone. Friends who thought they'd decide by morning's light have missed their chance and must just hold on.

I watch the news with tears streaming. My home is blowing away. My home is being crushed. I wait for news. I check my phone. I call numbers and leave messages that go unheard. Call me, I say to no one there. I hit end and stare at the phone. Wondering. Thinking the worst and hoping for the best.

Someone in Nashville quips, "Why didn't those people just evacuate? Didn't they know?" I become mute in everything I want to say.

~

I evacuated one time when it looked like a hurricane was coming in fast and furious and might land as a strong Four. My daddy was worried and called and wanted me to get out. Me and sister packed up two cars with my two little boys, two dogs, four puppies, one cat, and all the family photos I could carry. We got caught in the evacuation exodus that no one understands until they do. We were crushed in traffic, in the midst of the whipping wind as I tried to hold the car to the road. My brakes went out as I skirted limbs that came down crashing into the road. Tornadoes chased us all the way to my Aunt Kate's door up in Georgia. It was days upon days before we could get back. When we did, the National Guard was still in charge, the power was still out.

~

Getting over Hathaway didn't work. The storm turned and wiped out Mexico Beach, taking memories along the way. I walked there, ran my dog, picked up shells, collected stories. There, once upon a time, I loved a boy, roller skated, held hands.

Blown away.

My phone keeps ringing from an unknown number. Finally, I check messages and it's Cousin Deb reporting: "Hey man, I borrowed someone's phone. It looks like a war zone."

Later, I'll care about all that destruction, but right now I'm just glad to hear her voice. I start checking Facebook, searching for news from friends. Someone has posted asking if someone can check on their mother, brother, sister ... and I pray. Because it's all I'm left with.

The news, Facebook, the images. A drone is flying through what's left of my middle school. My high school is devastated. Everything has been flattened. Friends are surfacing with nothing left—but their very lives.

This one got us. This one hurt. This one changed the landscape of our childhoods, our neighborhoods and our lives. But it didn't steal all that was best.

My friend Frank Sundram posted on Facebook during another hurricane a reminder from the old movie *Starman*. When the alien is asked why he wanted to come to Earth he replied, "Unlike the rest of the Universe, the people of Earth are at their best when things are at their worst."

I relied on Facebook now more than the news that had seemed to move onto other stories, flashing political tidbits, Michael becoming a footnote— but not in my world. This was my only story. My old journalism professor, Charlie Wooten, posted something about the fact that at the moment no one was waiting on FEMA, they were walking the streets with chainsaws trying to help neighbors get out of their houses, and for that day no one was Democrat or Republican or flying different kinds of colors and flags. They were one people. They had become what they were all along and maybe didn't realize. Neighbors. Friends.

Survivors.

Time and time again, I read about people coming out of their homes, out of what was left of their homes, and linking arms to figure out a way to make it through another day. To share their water, their food. And then I saw the ultimate post about how someone was both wanting everything to get back to normal and hoping that it never did. That somehow the new normal would prevail. Of how they'd made new friends they would not have known who now meant everything to them.

Every critical image is still searing. Friends tell me, "You won't know your home anymore." I get it. Everything has changed. Devastation reigns. The trees are gone, the skyline not the same.

But then I saw a picture of a sunrise on the bay a friend posted, and I thought, there is that. Just that. And the reminder that the majority of the reports that still surface are shining examples to me of what the country needs now more than ever. That given the opportunity to rise, we will rise. Given the chance to love, we'll love.

I cling to this truth. In the survival against what might be the worst to come, we will prove in a million ways be our very best.

Pennies and prayers. They both count more than you know. Give what you can, where you can from the heart of who you are.

And, storm be damned, I'm still a native girl and I'm proud to be coming home.

~

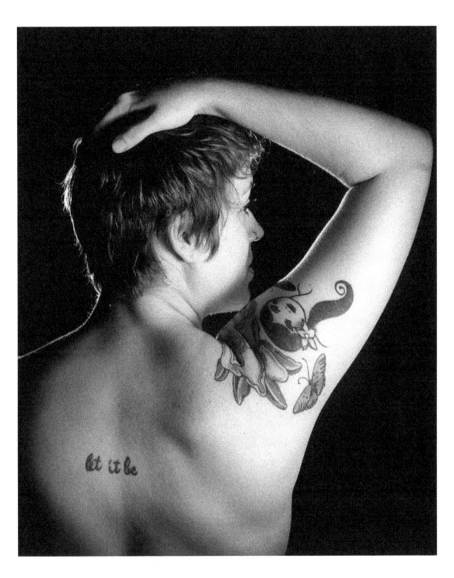

LET IT BE
KATIE CLARK
~

Stress eating is real
But not nearly as painful
As survivor's guilt

— *Lacey Phillips Maxwell*

~

FOR US THE STORM IS OVER
KATYA SABAROFF TAYLOR

For us the storm is over
for others, not, not at all
for them, it's no power,
no trees, no house, no cat.

For us the debris is gone
the lawn looks clean and new
the cat snoozes again on the picnic table

For them, standing in line for a handout
food, water, tarps.

For us, hot water again, and computers
For them, rotting floorboards, mold,
lost letters, lost pictures, lost beds.

For us the storm has passed
we who arranged survival in our
little hide-a-nook, on a comfy futon,
dreaming as the winds gusted
and then passed by.

For some the winds did not pass
so cleanly, so glancingly.

For some their hide-a-ways

were not sufficient,
there were holes in the roof
and suddenly stars, where the
dining room ceiling used to be,
and the trees snapped,
the waters poured down.

For us, it was like a strange dream,
from which we awoke, pleasantly,
to go about the work
of putting the plants back, the cherubs back,
the Buddhas back, the wind chimes back,
raking and wheelbarrow trips to
dispose of the litter. That's it.

For us the sun came out, the flowers waved.
For them, the storm continues,
through hard days, long nights,
fear, hunger, worry, homelessly
in limbo.

I don't want to trade places,
but I want to wonder,
what if it were me?

And then, who would I be?

~

WE DIDN'T LIKE THIS CARPET ANYWAY
SANDI MARLISA

It got to a point in the storm where all I could do was lie down on the floor while the world crumbled around me. Jesse, the former medic, was alert. He threw our dining room table in front of our glass sliding door. He moved the mattress in front of the window in the room we determined was the safest.

Then he lay down beside me and made me look at him. "Baby, we're getting a new roof out of this."

"Yeah," I answered. "We're getting a brand new roof."

"What color do you want it to be?"

"I always wanted to paint the trim of the house that dark brown/black so it looked like a cottage with the white stucco."

"That color it is."

He ran into the living room hearing a loud sound and suddenly rushed back in.

"Everything is fine!" He shouted, jumping over our bodies on the floor and running into the master bathroom.

"Then why are you screaming?!"

"It's fine!" He said, carrying out every towel we owned. "Just a few leaks."

I got up and chased him out of the room. Our house was pouring water from the roof and every pot we owned was catching the drips. It reminded me of that Winnie the Pooh movie when Piglet is trying to float out of his house in the pan, bailing water while his makeshift boat keeps sinking.

I froze and looked at Jesse.

"Baby," he said. "We're getting new floors out of this."

"Right," I answered. "We didn't like this carpet anyway."

"What color do you want it to be?"

"Grey tile that looks like wood, it's more modern ... and waterproof."

Jesse had an adrenaline rush and moved all our furniture, including my 500-pound-plus piano, to the middle of the floor. The water was pouring from inside the walls. I began throwing water outside and down the sinks as the pots kept filling, our house filling with an awful stale smell, our kids laughing in the bedroom.

We lay back down on the floor in our room while the worst passed. When the winds died down to a normal Tropical Storm, we opened the windows and stepped outside.

The air smelled of pine, like someone had just chopped down a million trees for a bonfire. The sky was an orange haze, filled with smoke and angry clouds. It was tragically brilliant and beautiful, the color you see in between dreams and nightmares.

Helicopters began to fly overhead, the elementary school alarm sounding off, the sounds of neighbors screaming through the debris, "Hey! Are you okay? Is anyone hurt? Can you sleep in your house? Do you have cell service? What the hell was that?"

Both ends of our block had several fallen trees.

Our neighbor's house across the street was no longer a house.

We were trapped.

The sky grew dark at 6:30pm and now there was nothing before us but a long, hot wait. We lit our candles, we locked our home and opened one window, hoping for a Fall breeze that never came.

A transformer blew with a loud "BANG!"

"Yeeyee!" A neighbor cried into the silence.

We laughed. "Yeeyee!" I answered back.

The night was hot, muggy and smelly. I couldn't sleep, so I looked outside and that's when I saw the stars in their brilliance. They blinked and one by one said, "Hello, we haven't seen you in a while."

"Hello," I whispered back.

I listened to the radio for information that was about as much as I had in the first place. The storm came, it was big, and—yes—your town is changed.

The dawn came and the birds started their singing. I watched a squirrel run up to our Pecan tree that lost all its leaves and branches, but still stubbornly stood like an arrow pointed towards the sky.

"My home lost its branches, too." I said to the creature.

Jesse stirred slowly in the morning and we looked at the roof.

A light kicked on in my mind, I smiled. "We have a tarp, we have nails, we have a ladder."

"I know," Jesse said. "I can't find the energy to get myself up there."

My husband stood strong through the storm and now energy was hard to come by.

"We're getting a new roof out of this," I said.

"Yes we are," he answered, and climbed on the roof. "This isn't enough tarp."

"We have the kids' inflatable waterslide. We can use that."

"You want to be the one to tell them?"

"No."

We did the work we could do, managed to find another tarp buried in our shed that was still standing, and then we ripped out our soaked carpets.

"How much water do we have?" Jesse asked.

"If we drink three 16oz bottles a day per adult, and two bottles per kid, we'll last 7 days." I answered.

"But it's so hot and we're working outside, we'll need more."

"I know. We won't be able to work this hard every day."

Then I had an idea.

"The white car has a full tank, but we can't drive it. We can sit in there during the hottest parts of the day and cool down. We won't have to drink as much water that way."

We moved into the white car and cooled off.

"Too bad this thing wasn't destroyed," Jesse said.

"Yeah," I answered. "But then we wouldn't have air conditioning."

"Do you know when it will rain?" Jesse asked.

"I can't check the weather," I said. "I can barely send texts."

"The tarp should hold okay. I'm worried about more water damage."

"We're getting new flooring out of this," I said.

"Yeah. Grey, it's more modern."

~

From the author: "Hope this can be useful for something other than my way of coping."

Temporary home
Sprung a small leak overnight
Just can't catch a break

— *Valerie Woods*

~

**WET PLATE OF CENTRAL PENTECOSTAL
MINISTRIES IN LYNN HAVEN**
ANDREW WARDLOW
(AndrewWardlow.com)

Publix parking lot
Water and WiFi baby
Ooh, yeah that's the spot

— *Britt Matthews*

~

BRANCH OF ENDURANCE
KAITLYN 'REI' KRETZER

Spin and twirl
Spin and snap
Branches of life
No longer intact

Sway and cling
Sway and break
The storm has come
Who will it take

One branch swings
Smacked side to side
Slapped back and forth
By the winds outside

But still it hangs
Still it clings
For its home tree
The peace it brings

No match for the storm
No match for the wind
That so desperately blows
To snap tree's strength

"Just a little longer"
The branch clings

"My father is swayed
Yet He still stands"

"That's enough
You've done your part
Rest easy now
This storm shall pass"

With all strength sapped
The branch lets go
The howling wind mocks
The little "dead" branch

The storm is gone
It has passed
The tree still stands
Branch lying nearby

"Good job my faithful servant
You prevailed against the wind
Now the storm has passed
Be bathed in sun's light"

Now at peace
The branch soaks in warmth
Dry and safe
Storm drenched no more

~

PERSPECTIVE
JUSTIN BUTLER

The elevator in the condo smells like stale cigarettes. The stench is that of the collective stresses all the temporary of tenants in this complex are experiencing after a few hours of strong wind completely restructured the reality they live in. One by one, exhausted passengers step off. Some carrying what groceries they could find, others covered in dirt and wood shavings looking forward to their first warm shower in days. I step off when we reach the top floor. I set my bags down and walk through my temporary home, out the back door onto the balcony overlooking the ocean to stargaze and attempt to find some perspective.

I'm here because a tree rudely decided to commandeer my home. I'm surprised the landlord allowed this to occur; as trees make terrible tenants. This particular tree wrecked the place as soon as it arrived and allowed many of its friends to pass out drunk in the yard. Hurricane parties are one thing, but this was just absurd.

It took me two days to learn of this intrusion, as the storm had rendered the roads to my house impassable. Even after those first 48 hours, I had to climb over trees for about a half mile to see my home. As I, filled with hurricane snacks, reached the halfway point and struggled to get over these obstacles, I met a man with long dreadlocks who warned me that the hard part was still up ahead as he bounded gracefully from the highest points of the downed pines. This encounter made me wonder if the storm had brought out some sort of magic in my community; and made me certain that I needed to put down the Pop Tarts.

After the harrowing trail reached its end, I finally reached my domicile. I assessed the damage, cursed the trees, saved the whiskey, and left quickly. I did not want to stay too long with the trees that had taken up residence. I hated them, but they greatly outnumbered me; best not to start any trouble.

So again, I travelled through the chaos. This time carrying a small bag of supplies and large bag of cat food. I'm a good dad.

On the drive back to my temporary shelter, I kept the windows down. The symphony of chainsaws serenaded with songs of community spirit, and the pine scent in the air reminded me that fall scented candles are about to go on sale and my girlfriend is going to bankrupt us. I see a chain diner restaurant has set up a truck delivering hot meals to families who have no access to the utilities necessary to cook one on their own. While I don't think giving people without access to water the runs is the greatest of ideas, I do sincerely appreciate the charity.

A few days pass and my little family—consisting of two cats and a pair of twenty-somethings trying their best—arrives at the condominium my job was gracious enough to locate for us. I carry the last of our bags up to the elevator with the cigarette smell, set the bags down, and here I am on the balcony as mentioned.

The stars do a lot to calm me. The vastness of our universe, so open and poetic. Yet, I have found no perspective.

Perspective is found in myself turning around and looking through the glass door. There I see my micro-lions and my best friend carrying on like normal. The box is different, but the contents remain the same. What is most important has survived, and everything else can be rebuilt.

~

STORM A'COMING
WAYNE GARRETT

First we heard:
"Expect a tropical storm,
It's a long way off,
And the gulf is warm."

Then came:
"Maybe, in the days to come,
It'll be a hurricane.
Perhaps, Cat One."

"Hey, Y'all:
This prediction's brand spanking new,
When that sucker gets here,
It'll be Cat Two."

"We never thought it would come to be,
But Hurricane Michael,
Is now Cat Three."

"Run if you can or brace up the door!
That ding bat storm,
Is a rocking Cat Four!"

And when it finally did arrive,
It was a blowing, going,
Category FIVE!

It made a mess and tore up the town,
But it didn't put,
The spirit of the people down.

They came out and went about,
Doing what was needed,
To sort things out.

Helping each other, stranger and friend,
And folks from all over,
Came to help us mend.

Adversity shows the grace of the family of Man,
When each of us,
Does the best we can.

And though it's a long trek back, it's one we'll weather,
Through work and faith,
And sticking together.

Panhandle Strong!

~

UNTITLED
CHRISTON ANDERSON
(Facebook.com/ChristonAndersonArt)

The dam of grief breaks open.

First unmuted words:

Belly churns
Teeth hurt
Heart burns
Doubled over
Punched in
Eyes refuse—
Each glance an earthquake:
Stripped, splintered, shredded,
Torn.
No and no and no and no.
And yet again,
Head shaking, violent no.

— *Johanna Rucker*

~

THE THERAPIST
S. BRADY CALHOUN

She had the best cookies.

Chocolate chip with that clear sprinkled sugar on top. Would have been even better warm, but the microwave was still in the part of the building being torn apart and rebuilt, and my allergies couldn't take the sting.

I made a point of going to her makeshift office in what had once been an edit bay and a point of making sure that certain coworkers saw me going. The guy who flipped out crying and screaming the day after the storm and begging to go work in Tampa so he didn't have to stay here. I wanted him to see it or at least hear about it.

Then there were the ones who had gotten quiet or angry or, the ones like me, who had tried to make a joke of it. Every day a new horror, was just an opportunity for a new joke.

"You believe this?" I said at one point. "We're living in Mogadishu."

Mogadishu stuck after that. And become my funny way of calling my hometown a war zone.

Ha ha.

So I walked in and had another cookie.

My Hurricane Michael diet allowed me to eat anything I wanted at this point. Down 15 pounds or so and at least one pant size. If living in the heat, drinking lots of water, and eating fresh fruit, home cooked meals and almost no fast food kept on, I had a real shot of going from fat man to reasonably healthy adult.

The therapist was the somewhat thin blond. A larger woman sat next to her, but whatever he function was (moral support or a second person in a room so it wouldn't be two people alone) all she did was smile, nod, and stay silent.

"I feel like I'm OK," I said. "But I was wondering what kinds of things I can expect."

Nightmares were common, she said.

None of those so far, I thought. I go home from work bone tired now, and with little television or internet options available I'm asleep by nine.

I can't remember now what the other symptoms were. But I didn't have any of them, and in my mind I probably wouldn't get them. There would be some things to look out for, sure, but I had beaten this thing.

"It was something," I said. "The roof of First Baptist flew off and landed on our roof. Then there was the smell of smoke, so we thought there was a fire."

My kids, which is how I think of the reporters who work for me, all broke down somewhere along that point and texted their families they loved them. Maybe it's a generational thing, but I never did that. I never thought, during the storm, that I would die.

"The scariest thing that happened," I continued, "was the damn idiot who ran down the street with an AR-15."

We had gotten over to First Baptist at that point and so we were just waiting for nightfall and for sleep.

The kids freaked out, screaming, and everyone ran inside. I went upstairs to the third floor. According to one of my co-workers, it was the fastest they had ever seen me move. I got a phone that worked and called our reporter at the EOC. She got me with a dispatcher and I explained what was going on.

"He's in a yellow jeep, he's wearing a red bandana," I said. "All of us from WMBB are here. Can you get someone over here?"

I don't know that, even then, with the prospect of a madman shooting up the church I was standing in, that I ever believed I would die. I did eye a door that led to somewhere else in the church and seriously considered if hiding would be an option.

"Doubtful," I thought. "If he goes room to room I'll just be trapped."

The police stopped the gunman on the street as he drove away in his jeep with a yellow blinking light. They talked to him for a minute and then let him go.

It was the next morning, when he swung back by, before I realized what he was. He pulled up as I was sitting in my boss' car charging my phone. I sat silently and couldn't breathe.

He hopped out of the jeep, moved some small debris out of the roadway, and then drove on.

"Oh my God," I said to myself. "This GI Joe jackass thinks he's helping."

Back in the edit bay, the therapist waited patiently for me to finish with my damage report.

"It sounds like you really went through it." she said.

"Well, I haven't had any of the symptoms you described, and I haven't really felt like anything was wrong," I said. "But I wanted to check in."

"That's good," she said. "It does sound like you have the things in place you need to deal with this. You have people to talk to."

"Yeah," I said.

I shifted in my seat.

"You know," I said. "There is this Facebook video. We shot it after the power went out. I was directing it. I haven't been able to watch it."

I just wanted to keep working. As long as we're all together and we were all working nothing bad could happen to us. So I discovered David's phone could get still get a signal, and we fought with the Facebook gods for 10 minutes until we were live.

They lit up Justin and Tom, and we started going again.

No power, hurricane still blowing. By God, we're gonna keep doing the news.

It lasted 15 or 20 minutes. My guys are the real deal with decades of experience. Tom Lewis is a damn legend.

And I never thought I would ever see all of them crying on camera.

Amy prayed and asked for prayers. I kept asking Justin, from off camera, how much longer did he think this would last. The worst part of it was over. Or would be. As long as Justin told me it was going to be OK, then it would be OK.

And eventually it was OK. The storm passed and we lived through the heart of it.

"You're going to have to watch it," the therapist said.

"Oh," I said. "Really?"

"Yes, it's a sign of PTSD, that you can't watch it," she said. "You are going to have to face it."

My left arm began to tremble.

"Well," I said. "Look at that. My arm is starting to shake at the idea of that."

"Right," she said. "It's something you will need to deal with. But watching it will make it better. You should call one of the trauma therapists and talk to them, and then build up to it. You don't have to just watch it cold turkey. … But you need to watch it."

I thanked them and my arm stopped shaking.

"I really appreciate you guys," I said. "God bless you."

I still haven't called the trauma people.

And I haven't watched that damned video.

And I'm fine. I'll be fine.

I'm fine.

~

PETRIFIED GRIEVER
ART AND POEM: MELINDA HALL

For too long,
She walked among the trees
Who grew too few in number.
Their slayers like bees.
Cutting, grinding, hacking, chopping...
Destroying their own means to breathe.

Many trees cried bloody tears too.
Sadly they begged and pleaded,
"Mother you can teach them," but she knew this to not be true.
They were so passionate, though,
That they offered to be Earth's Army of Light.
"We will win this battle against their Army of Darkness!"
Their cause being in the right.

Being so moved by their sacrifice,
Mother knew what she had to do.
Called upon the Winds of Change
And with voracious force they blew.
She commanded the Army
with great general-like airs,
So the trees bowed, broke, and fell.
For a time, the darkness would be quelled.

The Army of Light asked her, "Will the darkness return?"
"Oh yes," she replied, "but there are other Armies of Light, still asleep.
And we have hope that one day,
Our covenant, the dark shall keep.
Until then, I must move on
To awaken my giant sleeping one.
It will be difficult with such horrors,
It will explode, fire and flow, and blot out the sun.
Much more destruction must be done.
Then and only then will their world become one,
Our covenant fulfilled
Darkness be done
They will be the We
we are meant to be."

~

IN A WORD
DODIE HAYNES

I must have reached for my phone a thousand times in the last four weeks. Family and friends I hadn't heard from in months, some of them I hadn't talked to in years, suddenly wanted to know how I was doing.

I said I was fine. I assured and agreed that once everything settled down, I would give them a call. The truth was, I wasn't fine and they really shouldn't wait for a call that may never come.

And then, yesterday, I grabbed my phone, more out of habit than the need to connect; and there was an email from the college letting me know that their writing classes that had ended so abruptly after the storm were scheduled to resume on Friday.

"Yay!" I said to my dog that lay nestled between my phone and my lap.

I put the phone down, dumped the dog on to the floor and cleared my writing desk. With pen in hand, I stared at the blank page.

I knew I should just start writing something. Anything at all could lead to anything at all, but there were too many thoughts in my head.

I couldn't stop thinking about how my mom and I had decided to stay put for Hurricane Michael. How we poured our coffee and sat on the front porch awaiting Michael's approach.

It was a beautiful morning. We sipped leisurely and talked about everything but the worst-case scenario. I kept assuring her we would be fine. When the winds began to howl, I kept my phone in my hand, glancing nervously at the radar every few seconds. I promised her Michael would turn east, and he did. Wow, that was close.

With my pen still poised, I kept thinking about how afterward we sat in the dark and decided since the power would likely be out for a while we would go over to Freeport and spend the next couple of days with family. Why we didn't go there before the storm, I don't know, but we were relieved to have made it through and now we would just have to wait it out.

After a couple of days of wondering what was going on at the house, I let her sleep in while I went home to see if the power had been turned back on. I was happy to text her that it was and that I was coming back to get her.

"Yay," was her only reply.

Yay: a short utterance of emotion capable of standing alone. Yay: a three letter word that reads the same from any direction, like wow or mom.

"Yay." The last word she would leave me with before her heart stopped beating.

As I write this now, my pen struggles to make sense to the paper. All I can seem to write is—

Wow, I didn't see that coming.

Mom, I miss you so much.

~

UNTITLED
LOU COLUMBUS

~

"The tree that fell across our street and totaled my car.
This was taken after a group of volunteers took the first swipe at cutting it
into manageable sections."

PIECES
ERICA MCNABB FLOYD

Pieces.

Pieces of glass. Pieces of shingles.

Pieces of fences, siding and trees.

Pieces of broken dreams. Pieces of memories.

Pieces placed on the curbside to be whisked away and forgotten about.

But these are pieces of our lives. Pieces that have made us stronger, that give us hope. Pieces that formed relationships with people we would have otherwise never met.

Pieces that pulled families closer than they had ever been.

So as you are placing these pieces out to be removed and you see these pieces in piles along the roadside, remember these are not just pieces of debris.

These are pieces of our future.

~

MY HEART BREAKS TONIGHT
CAITLYN LUNDY

He thinks we're just on vacation...

My heart breaks tonight as I've spent the last few days giving small details as to what's going on at home. He just doesn't understand. I've been so impatient with this little guy through this process. He's been racing around and acting out because he knows something is off, but he just can't grasp the concept.

He doesn't know that he may not get to sleep with his mommy for a couple/several nights once I return home to work, leaving him with family over an hour away. He's convinced we're just on a long vacation checking different hotels out to see which ones we like most.

I wish we were on vacation. Taking him site-seeing and playing in the sun. I want to lie by the pool for several hours and watch his little freckles light

41

up like mine. I want to have days full of laughter. Actually enjoy the beach we've been looking at for the last three days.

Not worry that my bank account is virtually frozen. Apologizing to my server for being unable to tip her as well as I so wish I could when my card declined. Crying in the hotel elevator because who knows when I'll be this comfortable again. Unable to force myself out of my hotel room for more than mere minutes. And feeling guilty that some of my family is sleeping in half of a home.

It could be worse. I know that. They were just things, but they were things we've worked so hard for as a community. As a family. We will get through this. It will be years before we feel any real sense of normalcy or a sense of home. But we will triumph, right?

~

15 THINGS I LEARNED FROM MICHAEL
HANAN ELKOMY

1. Hurricanes are destructive and unpredictable.

2. Pack a bag of all your necessities in case your house is deemed unlivable and you need to find a hotel or friend.

3. Give in to that feeling of panic during the chaos while you're trying to shelter inside, listening to howling winds and crashing objects. And then give in to the helplessness you will feel after going outside for the first time and seeing 200-year-old trees uprooted (grass and all) lying on your lawn or on your roof. It's okay to feel those feelings.

4. All things can be replaced, except life.

5. You don't need as much stuff as you thought you did.

6. Electricity and air conditioning are luxuries, but not necessities.

7. Internet is a luxury. Be ready to live without it for a while.

8. You can flush a toilet using buckets of pool water or water from the bathtub that you filled during hurricane warning.

9. Have a generator, gas, batteries, flashlights, candles, clean water, medicine, and nonperishable food ready to last a week or two.

10. Candlelight is very romantic.

11. That hurricane deductible on your homeowner's insurance policy is not the same as your regular deductible, and is usually much higher.

12. When disaster happens, neighbors and even strangers come and help you.

13. It's only a disaster if you make it one.

14. You don't control anything. God is in charge.

15. That which does not bend will break. This includes trees, power poles, and people.

~

My children are well.
I feel guilty I'm not there.
I need to go home.

— *Rosemarie O'Bourke*

~

UNTITLED
CAROL SCHILLING
~

Blue tarps flap in wind
Will they fly off of our roof
Hard to really care

— *Ken Shaffer*

~

WHEN THE WINDS STARTED
ALEX SNOW

When the winds started blowing,
We didn't know they would be the winds of change.
We didn't know it would change more than the landscape of our community.
We didn't know they would change the hearts and minds of our neighbors.

When barriers came down,
We didn't know they would be the barriers of race and religion and lifestyle.

When trees fell,
So did the hate and mistrust so many had been holding onto their whole life.
We didn't know the things that had separated us for so long
Would come down in the path of this storm.
People who had never talked
Suddenly helped each other day and night.
People who were once so divided
Now stood arm in arm to rebuild.

When Michael came for us,
We didn't know how different things would be in his wake.
But they are.
Where buildings have fallen,
We have seen people rise up.

Where there was once animosity and selfishness,
There is now love and a willingness to lend a hand.

Where once we were blind,
Now we see.
We see that the spirits of people are good.
We see that in time of crisis,
People will come through.
We see that we are so much more
Than just neighborhoods and schools and attractions.

We are people helping people.
We are survivors.
We are strong.
And we are so much stronger together.

~

GRIDIRON GIFTS
JOHN GIBSON

"The power of a sports team in a community…it's almost indescribable."
— *Wendell Pierce*

It's easy to miss Vernon, Florida.

Even for those heading southbound on State Road 79, which connects the rural wilderness and farmland of Florida's Panhandle to the Spring Break mecca known as Panama City Beach, the tiny burg named after George Washington's historic Virginia home isn't the kind of place that stays ingrained in the memory long-term. Vernon is the sort of place in which you (maybe) slow down as you're passing through, so as not to get a speeding ticket on your way to the sugary white sands and gourmet seafood restaurants located thirty-five miles to the south. Odds are, if you're not in the driver's seat, and happen to instead be engrossed in your hand-held device while sitting on the passenger side, you're likely to not even become cognizant of the fact that you're driving through Vernon.

Yes, it's easy to miss Vernon, Florida … unless, of course, you're a hurricane named Michael.

While it would not be accurate to say that Vernon felt the full wrath of the storm that battered the Gulf Coast on October 10, 2018, there is plenty of evidence that Michael made his presence felt there. Down trees, power lines, house-bound residents unable to escape their dwellings, and storm-weary citizens without power and amenities that were previously an afterthought; all a testament to the latest display of Mother Nature's fury.

Perhaps even more indicative of Hurricane Michael's aftermath in Vernon, however, is the presence of helpers. From all over the nation, assistance in rebuilding Vernon, along with the greater Panhandle area, has come in the form of extra law enforcement officials on loan to the affected area, utility repair trucks, food, water, supplies, counseling services, and dozens of other entities making their human devotion felt through their donations and presence.

Blue Ridge High School out of Greer, South Carolina is one such entity.

~

To truly gain an appreciation for the significance and central theme of any story, you have to start at the beginning. For Vernon, Florida, and Greer, South Carolina, the beginning of their story is Summer 2018, just a few short months before both small, Southern towns were visited by two different major storms.

As the outset of the 2018 football season drew near, the Yellow Jackets of Vernon High School were faced with a dilemma: how to fill a significant hole that had been left in their schedule following another team's cancellation. In late July, second-year head coach Gerald Tranquille was put in touch with a school up in South Carolina which he had never previously heard of, and likely never would have played had the circumstances been any different. As fate would have it, however, this team also had an empty space in their schedule that matched Vernon's. Things moved quickly, and the Tigers of Blue Ridge High School in Greer were soon making plans to head roughly 400 miles to the southwest to play a team that they had never heard of.

…In a town that is quite easy to miss.

Fast-forward to September. Hurricane Florence bears down on the Atlantic coast, forcing evacuations and wreaking havoc on properties in the form of 100+ mile-per-hour winds, and floodwaters reaching upwards of 20 inches. Towns along the North and South Carolina coasts sustain catastrophic damage, as do small towns throughout the inland regions of both states.

Greer is one such town.

As families and communities struggled to pick up the pieces in Florence's aftermath, there was talk of cancelling the inaugural (and perhaps one-time) match-up between Vernon and Blue Ridge. However, to assume that the game actually was cancelled is to miss one of the fundamental truths about the South in general, and the Florida Panhandle in particular:

Jesus may be the soul of many Southern communities, but football is the lifeblood that runs through and connects them.

The game went on as scheduled, and the town of Vernon hosted their guests for two days, putting them up in a small Christian campground roughly ten miles to the west of Vernon's diminutive town square, where the Tigers stayed from the Thursday of game week until the following Saturday morning. The team and their coaching staff were fed, as well as given any comfort that the tiny town of Vernon could muster, and this by itself would perhaps warm the heart of even the most objective sports observer.

However, the story does not end there. The citizens of Vernon also took up donations of every sort and packed the vehicles of both the team and its weary fans, who had also made the cross-regional trek from the Palmetto State, with supplies and other necessities to take back to their weather-beaten communities. Pledges were made for both teams to rematch in 2019.

A rivalry was created on the field, and a friendship was born of it.

Fast-forward to less than a month later. Vernon is now in the throes of recovery following Hurricane Michael. As with everything in our day and age of technology and social media, ubiquitous posts announce updates about the status of the rebuilding and relief efforts; news about relief shelters, disaster assistance outposts, and personal updates on family and friends.

Amidst all of this information, there also surfaced a link to a website in which the Blue Ridge High community in Greer had organized their own relief effort for the town of Vernon.

Blue Ridge was giving back to Vernon; to the community which had taken them in after Hurricane Florence and allowed them to resume their lives with a degree of normalcy as their football team took the field against Vernon High; back to the citizens of northwest Florida which had showered them with relief supplies and goods only a month earlier.

The newfound friendship was growing, and has continued to do so as donations have poured in via the website.

~

If there is a moral to this easy-to-miss story, it's this: each year, it seems as though controversies within sports become more numerous, as well as more magnified. Whether it's discord generated over patriotic displays, public demonstrations, or even matters as superficial as how lucrative players' salaries should be, the screams favoring one side or another of a given polemic only seem to get louder by the season. And in the midst of it all, the rest of us grow more and more disillusioned and cynical as a result.

Perhaps that is why the newfound kinship between two high schools, previously unknown to each other and brought together by circumstance and two different displays of Mother Nature's fury, is so vital to our human experience. Perhaps amidst the cultural decay that too often monopolizes our consciousness, Vernon and Blue Ridge's commitment to serving each other and helping their fellow man can serve as a diamond-twinkle in the rough, from which we can learn a thing or two about community and giving back in times of need.

Indeed, if football is the lifeblood that runs through our communities here in the South, then perhaps we can take comfort in knowing that at least two of those communities are healthy and apt to endure whatever hardships may be on the horizon.

~

NEEDLEWORK SERIES

JORDAN KADY

~

Michael wreaked havoc
Some folks lost everything
We help each other

— *Charlotte Warnberg Moreau*

~

I AM WITH YOU
JENNIFER NELSON FENWICK

Who calmed the wind,
And stilled the waves?
Gave us strength,
In those first days?

Provided hope,
When there was none?
Renewed our faith,
With the rising sun?

Breathed His life
Into our lungs?
Cleared the way
For the work to be done?

Walks with us,
Down this broken road?
Eases our burdens,
Shoulders our load?

Never turns His eyes
From our struggles and our pain?
Heals our many wounds
Through the power of His name?

He was there through the storm,

Through the darkness of night.
He was there in the morning,
When the sun shed its light.

He was there when our eyes,
First beheld the destruction.
There when the tears fell,
From hearts torn and broken.

His presence is steadfast,
His mercy unending.
Trust in His promise,
This is just the beginning.

He will lead us without fail,
Down the long road ahead.
Turning all that's broken,
Into relentless hope instead.

Through Him we are restored,
Through Him we will prevail.
His unfailing love,
Will guide us through this hell.

For that is His great promise,
Renewed as each day dawns,
"Through trials and tribulations,
I am with you through the storm."

~

OCTOBER 26
HEATHER PARKER

Today I stood over the washing machine and peered in, trying to remember if I'd added soap already.

There were no signs. No clean scent, no suds. I'm sure I already added the soap?

Already half full of water, I'd loaded the washer with half-damp, half-crusty, stinky rags. Hurricane rags. We used them to sop up rain water that blew into the house and puddled in our dishes and in the corners, creeped behind cabinets and in computers.

I can't smell the clean scent of soap; nor the stink of hurricane rags. There's nothing. No thing. No sign.

There's a scent in the washer, but I can't smell it. There's a splinter in my finger, but I can't feel it. There's death and destruction beyond my street, but I can't see it. There's sadness in these Hurricane rags, but I can't feel it.

Is this tragedy? Is this catastrophe? I guess there's no clean scent in catastrophe.

A privilege, doing laundry. In a house with power and water and sewer. Are we 'survivors'? Will the reward for getting a new roof months before the storm be as strong as the punishment for not boarding up? If the windows hadn't blown, would the whole house have gone? Board up before or board up after.

It's dark in the house with less windows. Extra roof panels hastily screwed up to cover the gaping rectangular holes.

This is grief, isn't it? It snuggled itself in all cozy like.

I did so good this last 16 days. Doing the things. Fix the problems. Close the breech. Get the water. Dump the ice. Make it safe. Get the wet out. Save the treasures. Do the things. Toss the ruins. Remember all the things. Sleep with your car keys. Charge the phone. It works for 911. Feed the dog. Eat the food. Brush your teeth. Rest. Do the work. Don't get sad. Clean up the glass. All the glass. Don't get cut. Be careful. Watch for nails. Tetanus shots are free. Stand in line. Have cash. Check on the neighbors. Walk. Look. See. Charge the battery. Secure the house. Listen. Smell. Lock up your money. Don't get too hot. Do the things.

Did I add the soap? Why can't I tell?

This is grief, isn't it? It's snuggled itself into all my being, taken hold in every crevice, breeding like mold.

In my next life, I'm going to be a first responder. I'm good at that shit. If I was a first responder, I'd be leaving town right now. On to the next tragedy, to do my part, help the people, solve the problems, restore the order. I don't even know what the second wave people do.

Did I add the soap? What day is it? Is this the second wave? What next?

~

FLUID PAINTING
DON KEEN
~

People or buildings
What do we know more about
My building is ok

— *Wendi Garrett*

~

NEXT TIME
SAMANTHA NEELEY

There is a man holding a megaphone and he is telling us this was the judgment of god.

I don't believe him because I am still alive.

But I know my protest laws,

so I call them cops and let them know he's using an amplifier and blocking the flow of traffic for those who aren't.

The dispatcher thanks me and
I think she means it.

There are winds of 30 mph heading our direction and my coworkers stay home.

Usually only I am prone to unjustified panic, but today they will not leave their house or risk the roads and

I watch the trees shake and she meets my eyes when she says "I know."

I'm sitting on the living room floor, and my boyfriend asks me if we really need six cases of water,

the list of emergency stations that someone stapled to my door,

if we can put away the extra leash.

I can't make eye contact when I ask

"but what if we need them next time?"

(Nexttime.Nexttime?Nexttime?)

On day twelve I finally stopped apologizing when I hugged people because my mom had water and we had a gas can so I could shower
and even though it didn't wash anything away I could at least tell you how glad I was you were alive while smelling like vanilla instead of sweat and

Now I turn on my phone flashlight before I think to reach for the light switch.
I laugh about it and feel guilty for even having power.
Fourteen days is a long time but they're still living in tents down the road from my job and

Do any of us really have any power?

People keep saying they were "blessed"
and the inside of my cheeks hurt as my teeth sink in
and my mouth fills with blood and the words "what about those who weren't?"

Are we playing favorites now?

How do we justify luck?

It was wind, not some invisible hand, and you were lucky and I was lucky and we were lucky and that's terrifying

Because
Luck
Runs
Out

... and I'm angry.

Because there's only so much you can do to regain control and no one will call me back and there's a tree in my roof but not my ceiling and

I am guilty because I have nothing to complain about comparatively but no number of hot meals I hand out or friends' houses I pack up seems to offer absolution and what do you say when

I am scared. I am aimless. I am craving routine and normalcy, but I have these phone calls to make and this man to meet about a pile of dirt and—

(They have two tents now.
Maybe they're doing better?)

And what if it happens again?
And what about the people in those tents?

And when do you stop living in both the fear of the past and future, and how were those first few days the most I ever felt alive when I couldn't even tell you what road I was on

and who has water and will the trucks actually show up and how long will the battery packs last and does anyone know what's happening because I have no way to know and who do I call for that and how do you want me to send pictures (carrier pigeon or smoke signal) and is she supposed to be panting like that and have you heard anything from, do you know where they are and—

And there are no sirens anymore. Or buzzing of chainsaws. But I don't remember if my fan always sounded like that and I ask my boyfriend to turn down his video game because it sounds like wind and

I remember the trees snapping. One and another and another and another
The reoccurring popping of my yard and my ears and

And the impact. The way the house shook. I could feel the walls shaking but somehow I wasn't and

The way we pushed the couch in front of the door when we could see the world behind it and—

And how he told us to run so we pulled all the animal carries into one room and I tucked my head into my knees because the last thing the man on the radio said was "oh my god" and everything went silent and is this the end or just the eye because it's been four hours and I'm not sure but I don't know how long my heart can beat this hard

and how was it at the end that I finally thought to question if I was going to die and who do you call first and

And there is a man holding a megaphone and he's saying it's an act of god, and I roll my window up because I just want a fence again so my dog will stop peeing on the floor because that's not how things used to be—

—nothing is what things used to be.

But no one tells you that before.
And no one tells you how to prepare for after and—

And I was one of the lucky ones but

But luck runs out.
And what about next time?

~

WHO ARE THE DETERMINED?
WILLIAM HARRISON

You have probably heard of the uniquely skilled local surgeon who despite not having a hospital or an Operating Room and having received lucrative offers to move elsewhere is determined to help his people and a community he loves.

The mother of a 3-year-old who will wake up this seventh day following a week-old eviction notice, but she is determined to well care for her child and her pregnant twin-laden neighbor.

The favorite restaurant owner now serving in a school kitchen with his employees, determined to take care of his long term employees and rebuild his restaurant while rebuilding his destroyed home.

The city employee who clears a pathway to a gravesite in a city cemetery, determined to enable a mother to be buried by her husband.

The man who leaves his damaged medical office to meet with prospective contractors to rebuild his damaged church, determined to restore a space of sanctuary and worship for his congregants.

The Drug Court defendant, who offers a generator and refrigerator to the court to enable daily drug urine tests, determined that he will not succumb to the lure of his former downfall.

The mother, who scours in search of her children's friends, determined that if nothing else is going to be normal, friendship will be.

The group of friends who finally gather after three weeks, and who listen intently to one in the group who lost his home and his business but pays out of his savings to take care of his employees as he forgets to eat his hot meal, as he implores his friends because he is determined to save them all.

And to the one intently looking for the ones who fall through the cracks, who received a Facebook friend request from someone with no mutual friends identified by an uncommon name, who could just as easily been a foreign-based hacker, but the determined saw that it was a broken-English speaking single mother caring for a young child.

~

In some far-away place today, some boys will toss and kick a pigskin ball as they run up and down a beautifully manicured lawn. Tens of thousands will holler, scream and clap as numbers change on a board while they're dressed all in the same colors.

Not only will no one here see that once common pastime, we won't see the replay or even easily find the scores. The football, baseball, and election seasons ended a few weeks ago, as the Determined season opened.

~

Onward and upward my Determined friends and neighbors!

Thousands of Determinations will occur again today here, and I deeply and especially appreciate that you join my family — Determined.

~

UNTITLED
DANIELLE ASHLEY PIECHOWAIK
~

Chainsaw sirens scream
Constant generator hum—
Morning coffee blend.

— *Jayson Kretzer*

~

THOUGHTS IN THE AFTERMATH
KATHY GELLAR

A dirty, pink upholstered chair
sits awkwardly alone
at the foot of a driveway
waiting for a limo
to deliver hope

Sometimes the reality is
Humpty Dumpty's home
can't be put
back together again

A rain-soaked teddy bear
sits atop a debris pile
missing the embrace
of its toddler owner

News flash:
In our yard
brown bunny emerges from
beaten-down sea grass
at water's edge.
He survived!

~

Peeled back metal roof,
Like a sardine can. But no
Fish inside. Just lives.

— *Sarah L. Guillot Register*

~

A LITTLE WIND, A LITTLE RAIN
GREG RAY

A little wind, a little rain.

For years this has been my mantra for the many hurricanes and storms that threatened my hometown of Panama City, Florida. Living in a large brick home on a small hill twenty miles inland, even Opal had made little more than a nuisance of herself toppling the odd planter and random yard decor and layering our yard with a fresh bed of pine straw. Speaking to some concerned online friends on Tuesday I repeated my mantra to them.

We had been through Category 3s before. We were smart. We were prepared. After what was surly to be a milder storm than the weather jockeys were predicting, we'd clean up and be back to normal by the weekend. As I left work Tuesday afternoon I remember thinking I should have set the garbage can inside.

Oh well. A little wind, a little rain.

Wednesday morning I watched the reports and the live beach cams. I made funny comments to my fellow viewers about the red thing that floated ashore behind Schooners, a local restaurant. I watched the waves crashing over the city pier. I thought "Wow, the beach is going to get pounded."

I checked in with my concerned online friends. "We'll be fine," I wrote. "This isn't our first rodeo."

I joked with Mom how hurricanes are like Christmas: All the family comes over, you light candles, you eat all the good food in the freezer, and you anxiously await the arrival of your special visitor. I was having a good time enjoying the day off and the break from the mundane. I was even a little disappointed that only hours away from landfall Michael was still only a Category 2 and was predicted to hit further east from us.

As the weather worsened, I thought I should put the dog in our concrete block shed but the rain had started then so I put her in the laundry room instead. I played on my phone. I checked Facebook. I wondered if UPS would deliver on Thursday. The lights flickered a few times then finally gave up.

"There she goes." Dad said.

Our first indication that things were bad was when the wooden tool shed disintegrated.

Mom and Dad watched it go standing in front of one of the three sliding glass doors that face our backyard. The shed and its contents including a rather large air compressor and an imposing table saw all vanished into a swirling vortex like a malign magic trick. It was there and then it wasn't. Now you see it. Now you don't.

For his next trick, Michael slammed our front door inwards. This was truly amazing since moments before the door had been locked, latched, and bolted. We managed to close it against the opposing wind but Michael wasn't interested in our door anymore, he had moved on to our trees.

There was a crash from above like a truck being dropped on the roof. We looked around and up, confused. We heard water dripping. Something had hit the roof. We looked outside and saw the largest pine in our front yard had been sheared off about ten feet up from the roots and was now taking a nap on top of us. One of it limbs waved at us slyly through a ragged hole in our dining room ceiling.

"Okay Mom, Dad, we're moving into the hallway now." I said.

We crouched and lay listening to and feeling the war raging around us. In trying to describe it later I told my online friends, "Imagine lying between a pair of railroad tracks while a freight train runs over you for an hour." It's a ceaseless roar and soul-jarring vibration that shakes flesh, bone, and mind.

Inexplicably I still had cell service, so I watched as the eye crept past just to the east of us. We were in the western eye wall in a thick red band signifying the most intense winds. We weren't even to be blessed with a few moments relief from the eye. The eye was looking elsewhere.

I messaged my friends just before I lost service. "It is bad. Trees down on the house. Roof leaking. We are all sitting in the hall. Pray if you believe or not."

I've always struggled with the concept of fearing God. I was never really a God fearing person. Why should I fear God? I loved God and He loved me. He protected me and guided me. He was my Father and I was his errant but faithful child. To paraphrase Mick Dundee, God and me, we were mates.

The noise around us was deafening. Each new crash caused my heart to pound harder against my chest and sent electric tingles to my toes and fingertips. I could literally smell our fear. We were sweating pure adrenaline. I knew that if the storm didn't kill us a heart attack would.

"Please God," I prayed, "Please, please, please."

Huddled in that dark, stinking hallway I feared God.

~

Some believe Hell to be an eternal anguish of no escape for those caught in its grasp. For us, it was about 50 minutes.

~

Eventually we became aware of a lessening to the fury around us. We rose to find ourselves in a world completely unrecognizable as the home we had occupied for nearly 35 years. There were no familiar landmarks in our yard. No friendly 3-story birdhouse. No bed of day lilies meticulously tended by my mom. No mailbox. No driveway. There was only a madness of twisted limbs and detritus.

We meandered around outside like shell-shocked refugees from a POW camp, confused and disoriented. Two of our sheds were completely gone. The concrete block building where I had considered sheltering our dog had a hole in one wall big enough to drive a truck through. Apparently the wind had entered under the eaves and blown the wall and the door out like a bomb. We couldn't see the street but we could see the creek which had previously been hidden behind a quarter mile of dense woodland.

Mom cried. Dad shuffled around the wreckage in shocked silence, his senses overwhelmed, his circuits temporarily blown.

Some of my family members were in Callaway when the storm struck. I tried to contact them but there was no phone service. I sent a text anyway letting them know we were alive and asking them to contact me as soon as possible. I hoped they would receive my message when the phones were working again.

The neighbors began to gather in our street which had become an unrecognizable tangle of fallen trees and power poles. All of us shared the same stunned expressions. We spoke together in reverent tones like strangers at a wake. Some joked uncomfortably then quickly hushed, embarrassed and surprised by their own levity. We shared our stories, each one more fantastic than the previous. All of them seemed to share a common thread: "If this or that had happened we would'a been dead."

Before the storm we had fifteen or twenty large pines in our front yard. One of them was still napping on the roof of our dining room. I eyed the three remaining trees there. If any of them had fallen they would have landed square on top of us in the hallway and yes, odds were we would be dead.

That night there was still no word from my family. I was still praying, "Please God, please, please." None of us slept much. The reek and the heat and the lingering terror were too much. There were seven of us and two useable beds. There was a big ugly stain on the ceiling of my bedroom where water was gathering. I moved everything away from the drips and thought, "It'll be okay."

About 2 a.m. Thursday morning I thought I should plug my phone into my computer to charge. I went to my bedroom to retrieve my charger. As I turned to leave the room the ceiling decided it had had enough and collapsed sending an avalanche of drywall, insulation, and storm water into my bedroom. After the horror of the day, I simply stared at it a few moments and closed the door.

~

Thursday morning we awoke from our half-sleep to the sound of chainsaws. A neighbor and his buddies were clearing our driveway. We hadn't gotten along with this neighbor very well before but here he was sawing and hauling and sweating so we could get our cars out. Phones were still out, so I listened to the car radio for news of the situation. Callaway had been one of the areas of town hardest hit by the storm. I waited for a death toll which I reasoned must be in the hundreds if not thousands but there were no numbers being given. Only sketchy reports of massive destruction throughout our area.

"Please God. Please please please."

My brother lived in a mobile home about a mile from us. He had stayed with us during the storm and was anxious to see what remained of his home and his daughter's who lived next door. We drove as far as we could, then walked, crawled, and climbed the rest of the way. When we reached the creek beyond where he lived we realized we had gone too far. Amazingly we had not recognized his home of thirty-odd years when we passed it on the street. We turned back and finally glimpsed it through the fallen trees. By some miracle his trailer and his daughter's were completely unharmed except for a single limb which had broken through a window into my brother's spare bedroom. Behind his daughter's home we uncovered another miracle. Their camper was tilted sideways on two wheels supported solely by one corner of the camper top which was resting against the trailer's rear sliding glass door. The glass was unbroken.

~

I was frantic to hear from the rest of my family in Callaway. Finally I decided to try to drive to their apartment. The usual twenty minute trip took us two hours of inching along dirt back roads and gridlocked highways through a nightmare landscape of unbelievable destruction.

The entire county had become a surreal sideshow of the grotesque. There were ancient oak trees uprooted and tossed carelessly alongside mobile homes that were seemingly untouched. We saw entire forests of pines with their top halves cleanly sheared off as if God had decided to give the world a crewcut. Familiar streets were unrecognizable, their landmarks covered in debris or erased entirely. Many times it was impossible to recognize where exactly we were.

In town we discovered more wonders. We saw a mattress store squashed flat, its roof resting on a bed of broken glass and twisted metal and I assume mattresses. I thought that perhaps in this case the safest place to be in a hurricane is not under a mattress. We saw a semi truck lying on its side with the rear end of the trailer blocking one lane. I hoped no one had been attempting to drive in the middle of the storm but the alternative, that the truck had been blown here from some nearby parking lot, was unimaginable. Not far from there we saw a billboard supported by an enormous steel upright lying gently down on the Waffle House beside it; the upright now a downright

Finally we reached my family's apartment building and our first reaction was not good. There were trees on many of the buildings and some were missing their roofs and outer walls. We parked as close as possible and walked the rest of the way. My family was not there. I saw through their windows that their apartment at least seemed mostly intact although a limb had broken a window into one child's bedroom. It was hopeful but not completely reassuring.

The family that was with me wanted to check on their mobile home so we drove there next. The metal awning which covered their porch had been taken along with a sizable chunk of the roof and wall. Their bedroom was unreachable due to the remains of the battered roof blocking the hallway so we gathered what we could and left.

I dreaded seeing what remained of my business but it was the final thing on our list so we drove there last. My partners had arrived minutes before us and were standing in the parking lot in front of what looked like the setting of some violent video game — Comic Emporium: The Apocalypse. I stepped out of the car and gaped at the carnage. The front door and one window was gone, Hanging bits of fiberglass insulation waved at us through their ragged openings. The six foot awning which had previously ran the entire length of the building was now an unrecognizable heap of brick and metal and wicked looking nails clawing out of shattered wood. The brick columns which had supported the awning were all either leaning against the building or lying shattered on the ground amongst the ruins. Inside it was worse. Most of the front half of the store had been blown into the corner behind the counter where I had spent the majority of my days and many of my nights for the previous eighteen years. A soggy mound of ceiling tiles, insulation, hanging files, and comic books crouched there like the sad horde of a very poor dragon. The ceiling was a spotty crossword puzzle with dangling bits of wire and sagging supports. Water dripped in a dozen or more places.

Overwhelmed, I stepped outside as the first tears came.

I stood in the parking lot of that broken comic and game store as the horror of the last twenty-four hours crashed down on me and my soul buckled. I have never felt such loss and desperation not just for my business but for my world which I knew could never be the same.

The town I was born in, grew up in, and most likely would die in was gone, taken by the wind and the rain just like our old wooden shed. For the first time in my life I was utterly lost and devoid of hope and I cried in mourning for myself and my world. It was at that moment that the missing family I had been searching for rolled into the parking lot.

I embraced and kissed each one of them while sobbing with relief. It was ok. We were alive and nothing else mattered. When the rest of my family and I were in the hallway listening to our world disintegrate around us I had not prayed "Please God, save my business. Please God save my house." I had prayed "Please God save my family. Please God, please, please, please save my family."

God had listened.

God had answered.

~

An atheist friend asked me, "You believe in God, how do you explain things like this? What good could possibly come from something this tragic?"

I explained that the world is not always a good place and that bad things sometimes happen to good people but God sends a lot of good into the world as well. I told about the difficult neighbor who cleared our driveway. I told about another neighbor whose last conversation with my dad had been to cuss him out for agitating her constantly barking dog. The morning after Michael she had asked him how we were and had even said "God bless you."

I told about the three trees that didn't fall, the family pet that was alive because I decided to put her in the laundry room instead of the concrete block house, and the miracle of my brother and niece's unharmed trailers. I told about the thousands upon thousands of people that came to our town afterwards to hand out food, water, diapers, and various other necessities.

One of my heroes is Mister Fred Rogers, whose mother told him in times of disaster look for the helpers. There will always be helpers. In the days following Hurricane Michael, I saw an awful lot of helpers.

It's been nearly a month since Michael came to Panama City and life is still uncertain. There's power now at our house, but the phone service is shaky so for now we stay at a cousin's house where we can conduct the necessary business of reassembling our lives. Some of my family was forced to relocate due to their jobs no longer existing but they are not far and they seem to be doing well. The shop remains in ruins. There's still no power, the interior is in shambles and the parking lot looks like a battlefield. Every day I work to restore it to a semi-livable state but the road to recovery looks long and full of shadows.

Yet there is hope as old friends and customers lend their encouragement and support through fundraisers and donations. We will get there. eventually.

When I was a kid, I used to have nightmares of being lost in maze-like buildings while being chased by some unseen menace. Those dreams have returned, except now I find myself trying to escape ruined cities and buildings while dark clouds gather around me. I know that in time this too will pass, but for now part of me is still cowering in that hallway waiting for the nightmare to be over and for life to return to normal. Panama City will never be the same, but I'm certain we will find a new normal and a new kind of good and the horror of Hurricane Michael will eventually fade from our memories like a passing storm.

A little wind, a little rain.

~

Let's play Pick Up Sticks
Anyone have a Bobcat?
Vroom goes the chainsaw

—*Valerie Woods*

~

BEAUTIFUL SUNRISE
DAWN PHELAN MANN

~

"A beautiful sunrise I would not have been able to see if I still had a back yard."

Trains, roofs, metal bill boards,
Trees, trees, trees, trees, trees, trees, trees.
All blown down by wind.

— *Sarah L. Guillot Register*

~

I'LL MAKE MY WAY OUT THERE
AT FIRST LIGHT
TESA BURCH

There are some trees you can shake,
and launch black birds across the sky.
Small, a child could grab a limb,
and sprinkle leaves all far and wide.

Then there are those it takes machines to move,
I grew up among *these* pines.
Sturdy, long leaf, sons of god,
Easy 75 feet high.

My pines, thousands of them,
My Florida,
My East Callaway Heights.

I heard they weren't doing so well
They had foolishly hunkered down in the center of an eye,
Outside.
They were first hand testimony to a wind so hard it had glowed white,

October 10, dawn, day, night.
I had to ride out to see them,
had to know they were alright.
They have been looking out for me my whole life.

When I arrived, every neck I saw was turned

Not red,
Just over

They had fallen on my childhood home and held my father tight,
Some twisted,
Some like a severed spine.
Some bleeding sap
Some telling lies
Some whispering "fuck mike"

All of them.
ALL OF THEM

Bent and broken down to size,
And hopelessly their crowns looking me right in the eye.

I never thought I'd see the day when I stood between them and the sky.

~

.

I'M NOT EVEN SURE
KIM MIXON HILL

I'm not even sure where to begin when it comes to Hurricane Michael. Everything is still so fresh and raw, and there are so many people who lost everything. All I can do is tell it from my experience, because that's the only way I know how to express it.

I have lived on the Gulf Coast my entire life. Often, people wonder why we live in an area prone to hurricanes. Well, let me tell you a little about the Gulf Coast of Florida.

We have some of the most beautiful beaches in the world. Miles of sugar white sand, emerald colored waters, and a diverse mix of marine life. From dolphins and sharks to manatees and sea turtles – I've seen them all. The skies are sunny and blue, although in a second that can change; the heavens will turn dark and the rain will pour. To me, that's the most beautiful of all.

The Gulf Coast has a mix of people as diverse as its fauna, flora, and marine life. There are people here that have spent their entire lives in one place, there are millions of tourists from all over the world who descend upon the area, and we're home to a variety of celebrities—from Emeril Legasse to Anne Rice—not to mention those who just enjoy visiting. But we're not Hollywood. We're down home, friendly, and you'll find the best stories from a diner waitress, an oyster shucker, the local artists, the people who work in the hospitality industry, or an 80-year-old woman you meet at Piggly Wiggly.

There are smaller stores that have been in business for as long as I can remember, yet you will find state-of-the-art condominiums along the same stretch of beach. You'll see tacky buildings that have garish paint colors and beautiful Art Deco homes and townhouses, all combined into an eclectic mix of color and style.

You'll find some of the best Southern cooking from your family, friends, or even your next door neighbor and can eat fresh seafood that was swimming in the Gulf of Mexico just hours before. And if you like both southern cooking and seafood—I make an awesome shrimp and grits.

Speaking of Southern cooking and family, my parents had always evacuated for hurricanes. My mom would gather up her prized possessions (her photo albums) and we'd get in the car and head to Dothan, Alabama. As I became an adult, we never had to evacuate because the storms that did affect us were nothing like this one. Sure, we rode out Hurricane Opal, but that was a category three and didn't hit us head on. Keep in mind that we have never had a storm like this in our area—ever.

People often wonder why people stay for a storm, but this one got strong fast and yes, we were prepared with flashlights, candles, water, dog food, canned food, a battery powered radio, and all the usual things, except for Vienna Sausages because those are just gross. But no one knew it would turn into the powerhouse that it became.

Back when the storm was just a small one, we discussed with our neighbors how we'd all leave if it got too big, but at the time it was coming in as a category two. Eventually, we were under an evacuation notice but for the storm surge only, which never reaches my neighborhood. So again, many people stayed, including us.

By the time it was coming in stronger, it was too late to evacuate. We are surrounded by bridges, which close if the winds get up to a certain miles per hour and that can be as little as 45-50 mph. We could have gone up Highway 231, which was congested with traffic while thousands of others headed out of town, but no one wants to get caught in a hurricane while on the highway. So along with our dogs, we hunkered down as they say, and prepared for the worst.

As it turns out, nothing I have ever experienced could have prepared me for Hurricane Michael. For hours, I lay in bed with my dogs and prayed. The winds were so strong I was scared to even look outside—and this comes from someone who loves storms, including the smaller hurricanes of the past. Usually you will find me taking some poorly made videos of bad weather but this one wasn't your usual storm.

I could hear large objects hitting the house and heard the trees falling on our neighbors' homes. In fact, I heard when our backyard neighbor's large sycamore tree hit their house. Fortunately, they yelled out a few curse words, not cries for help so we knew they were okay. Not as if we could have ventured out to help them anyway. I used to love listening to the breeze rustling the leaves on that tree. It's been around for decades and now it's gone.

As I lay in bed, I would press my hands against the walls and I swear to you, I could feel them "breathe." It was the most terrified I have ever been, and I thank God that I survived.

When the eye crossed over, I knew we had to go through hours more of the same thing. We'd lost power, we'd lost phone service. There was nothing to do but wait, pray, and hope.

After the storm was over, we went outside and it was wonderful to see our neighbors out, some we had never even met, checking to see if anyone needed help.

Our close neighbors had a tree on their roof, along with their carport upside down on that same roof. And the church that has been in our neighborhood for decades was decimated. That is just some of the immediate damage we saw and then I saw my own house.

The entire backyard was gone, the roof was severely damaged, we had water leaking into the ceiling, the entire privacy fence is damaged or in some cases, missing entirely. The porch posts blew away, the satellite dish tore off part of the roof, and trees we'd have for years are twisted – that is, the ones that remain. All of the storage sheds were gone, with years of memories strewn throughout the yard along with tools, the Christmas tree and decorations, and ironically, a brand new generator.

After the storm, we sat all night listening to the radio about the devastation and hearing some of the stories from people who could call in, or the DJs who had weathered it out at the station. It was hot, it was dark, and it was scary, but just hearing a friendly voice made us feel that we weren't alone in the world.

One bright spot was going outside and seeing the Milky Way from the house; something we can never do because of the light pollution. The other thing you notice after the power goes out all over town is how quiet it is. I remember in *The Stand* by Stephen King that after the epidemic had affected most of the population, it was so quiet that Frannie could hear Harold using his manual typewriter from far away—it's almost that quiet other than a stray vehicle or the sound of a generator.

We've since started picking up the pieces. We are extremely fortunate and although we have damage to our home, we know people who have lost everything.

I've seen the best come out in people and the worst, but I believe that these trials don't work that way—either you were a good person to start with or you weren't. A hurricane doesn't make you suddenly become a person who will try to cheat people on a roofing job and a natural disaster doesn't make you suddenly care about your neighbors and how they fared during the storm.

Overall though, I know our area is filled with good people, just like the heroes from all over the country who came to help. Whether they brought supplies, helped connect power lines, or worked clearing debris—it's not just a job. It's being there for those who need it.

The entire landscape has changed—we heard that in some places, 95 percent of the tress are gone. Buildings that have been around for a hundred years are gone, places we've visited for years are closing because of the damage, and you can even get lost in your own neighborhood because nothing looks the same.

While this section of the Gulf Coast may never be the same, we will persevere and rebuild. My beloved Mexico Beach has been leveled, but I can only hope that it comes back even stronger. My hometown of Lynn Haven was one of the worst hit areas yet I know that they are resilient and it will grow into what I once knew. Panama City, where I live is in shambles but again, I know that it will flourish and prosper eventually.

We are strong and we will not let this storm define us.

~

"Hurricane Michael was the third-most intense Atlantic hurricane to make landfall in the United States in terms of pressure, behind the 1935 Labor Day hurricane and Hurricane Camille of 1969. It was also the strongest storm in terms of maximum sustained wind speed to strike the contiguous United States since Andrew in 1992. In addition, it was the strongest storm on record in the Florida Panhandle, and was the fourth-strongest land-falling hurricane in the contiguous United States, in terms of wind speed."

~

UNTITLED
LENA ROCHELLE CROWE
~

Every street a new tear
Lost on my own street at night
Will we find our way?

—*Wendi Garrett*

~

HUNKER (DOWN)
MICHAEL A. DAVIS

The storm surge waves are growing
and this house is way too old.
Tornadoes sound like freight trains—
God, I wish we'd hit the road.

But that's just wishful thinking,
the time to leave has passed.
If I knew how to hunker, brother,
life would be a gas.

The wind just took the neighbor's roof,
I'm sure I heard somebody yell.
I'd love to run right over there
and find them doing well.

But that's just wishful thinking,
the truth is dark and cold.
If they'd known how to hunker.
I'd get to watch them folks grow old.

The radio's gone silent now,
and the banshee wind sounds blue.
My pretty wife, love of my life,
just whispered "I love you."

And I'm filled with wishful thinking
about all that could have been.
If I'd known how to hunker down,
and beat this God-damned wind.

~

Water for washing
Our pots, pans, souls and hands
FEMA baptism

— *Britt Matthews.*

~

A RUN-AWAYER'S PERSPECTIVE
WENDY LEWIS

It was the day after my birthday, and everyone was starting to get all panicky. Everyone meaning the upstanding, news-watchers of my community; panicky meaning that all of the bread and water was being swept off of the grocery store shelves in broad, sleeve-length sweeps.

Not only bread and water, but also chips and beer. If there is anything people want during a hurricane, it's chips and beer. You'd think nobody cared if their entire existence got smashed into a million tiny shards, as long as they had greasy Doritos residue on their lips and an alcohol-induced fog blanketing their brain.

The whole city was basically dashing through Wal-Mart in a daze, wondering what they might need "if this thing gets really bad." A flashlight. Batteries. Toilet Paper. Who really knows? But you buy stuff so that you feel like you're prepared. That's what everyone did.

This particular hurricane was named Michael, and it had been making its way up the Gulf of Mexico for days, wrapping a firm, cloudy vortex around its neck as it crept, like one of those ridiculous infinity scarves I hate so much. A Category 2-inching-toward-a-Category-3 hurricane was predicted to be approaching, which was not all that unusual. I had already been though a handful of storms in my 20-year Florida residency, and although they could be intense and even mean loss of power for a few days, the ones I had experienced mainly amounted to a ton of rain and wind.

But this storm was on path to arrive right at my front door, and it appeared to be strengthening in strides. This was unusual.

When the mandatory evacuation call went out, I was reluctant to leave. Jesse, my husband, wanted to drive directly to my sister's in Georgia, but the 6-hour drive seemed excessive when we'd be back in just a day or, at most, two. I dragged my feet through the packing process, reluctantly picking out a few comfy "travel outfits," since I'd basically be in the car the whole time — *gah*. I'd never been a fan of road trips, and taking a lengthy one simply to turn around the following day annoyed me. It was messing with my "normal," a bland but essential status only days later we'd all realize we were more attached to than our shadows.

We arrived in Atlanta late Tuesday night. My wonderful, genuine sister opened her doors and let us cram ourselves into her busy, peak Fall schedule without hesitation. She even had outings planned.

Wednesday around 10 a.m., we headed to a Hindu Temple, "the largest outside of India," my sister expounded. She was always scouting out unusual and (if possible) free activities to enrich, and they usually did.

Wispy clouds seeped like veins through the gray sky as we approached the prominent building, the outermost bands of the buzz-saw storm wreaking havoc some 300 miles below us. The weather channel reported that the hurricane's landfall over our hometown was now imminent. Feeling hopeless, I slipped my flip flops off and stepped inside the temple.

The inside was gorgeous: exquisitely carved in perfectly symmetrical, kaleidoscopic designs, like walking through a palace made of alabaster lace. Men, even boys, were invited to sit on the floor near the front of the Sanctuary; women were seated behind. My unwitting children exchanged quizzical eyebrow lifts at this arrangement, but sat in their designated areas without protest. Men on either side of the room performed some kind of full-bodied bow.

"It looks like they're practicing the worm," my daughter giggle-whispered.

"Shhh," I replied, shooting her the mom-warning look.

I followed the regulars through their rituals: A woman carrying a candelabra lit with candles wove through the congregation. Each person kneaded their hands above the flames, gathering whatever magic they exuded, and then washed it over their hair; like a lion stroking its mane. I followed suit, praying as I lathered my hair with smoke.

"Please protect our community. Please, please keep our family and friends safe," I implored genuinely and deeply, and I didn't feel weird, blowing my prayer into that beautiful, crocheted handkerchief of a chapel. Every version of God amounts to the same idea, to me.

I spent the remainder of the day combing through news stories and Facebook posts, craning to see a video that showed a segment of my neighborhood; a view of my road. Footage near my home and business depicted rooftops peeling away like scattering dandelion seeds. I envisioned my home flooded, or slashed in two by a tree, and tried to brace myself for my possible new reality. It seemed scary, but foggy and unknown, like a woman in her third trimester trying to imagine what parenthood will really be like.

The following day, a friend who had stayed in Destin during the storm drove into my neighborhood and took some photos of my home and business. "I'm not gonna lie," she told me, "your house has some pretty serious damage. Trees are down everywhere. Your business looks like it might have some issues, too."

It was on the "lighter side" of the news being delivered in those first days following the storm. Literally thousands of others were being notified of crushed roofs, walls that had blown right off, cars smashed by trees—an endless inventory of decimated existences.

Here's what happens in the days after a hurricane, if you're one of the lucky ones. I'm talking about people like me, who, fortunate enough to be able to heed the mandatory evacuation order issued for my area, now live with the heavy guilt of having run away, tail between my legs, only to return once the power and water was back on; once toilets were flushing.

Nobody can accurately picture the horror of the hours and days immediately following the storm, if you didn't live through it. Those who did are certain to ask, "Did you stay?" Answering that you evacuated, "because I was in a mandatory evacuation zone" you over-explain, earns you a sparkled, scrutinizing stare tinged with envy, but also with chin-lifted resentment. There's an enormous gap between the stayers and the run-awayers, and those who stayed hold a secret only they can share.

For despite the current nightmare of living in the wake of destruction, they've walked away from death, and have seen a glimpse of eternity unlike anything I've experienced. I envy it in a strange way. And I think they might look down on me for not knowing what they know.

Several days, maybe a week, after the storm, you start to have weird conversations. Like, almost constantly. A strange new vocabulary emerges: "How did your home fare?" And the unanswerable: "How are you doing?"

This one quickly became a joke to me. "How are you doing?"

"Well, my home and business just got destroyed, so... how are you?"

"Oh, same here. But my mom's place is mostly intact, so we're sleeping on her couch for a few weeks while we figure out what's next. Aren't we lucky?"

"Aren't we? So blessed."

Nobody here wants to seem ungrateful, which is respectable, considering a broken but livable home is a luxury in these parts that many would envy. So we gather among the trash heaps that now line every neighborhood street and all talk about how lucky we are; so thankful.

And during those first weeks, buried deep within those spindly, clawing heaps of branches, a light springs forth, massaging the weary shoulders of all those gathered among the rubbish with hope, camaraderie, and community. Why are tidy, perfect looking porches often such cold, sterile meeting places in comparison to these Elk Lodge gatherings happening among the fallen pines?

Some of first defiantly starlit nights after the storm have beautiful, silver linings. There are newfound connections. Neighbors you've lived next to for years without truly knowing are now dear friends. Shared wine and grilled-out dinners abound. A new schedule is set by the planets. The everyday accessories of life are stripped away, until a makeup-free, bathrobe-clad community gathering is the norm. I'm delighted by this aspect of it. But the joy is quickly overshadowed by the overwhelming tasks ahead.

Sympathy is as hard to come by as gasoline. Of course, everyone is sorry to hear about your damaged roof, your destroyed business, your totaled car. But then, they've got their own destroyed situation to deal with; how can they go fund your life? It looks like a total loss from here; better file with FEMA.

Less than a mile away, separated only by a concrete bridge, life is worse. Much worse. A civilized society, even in the poorer-American South, is still one addicted to the internet, electricity and water. Take these basic privileges away and watch: the fragile humans quickly turn savage as hope and drive runs dry.

"Rattled" is one good way to describe the locals wandering up and down the roads, picking at the piles of debris, searching for items to help salvage their lives.

A *Lord-of-the-Flies*-ish division begins to segregate the townies and the beach-bums. Catty comments regarding the fluctuating demographic on the beach barely disguise disgust. Folks from over the bridge are defensive at the beach-people "in la-la land, like nothing ever happened." In truth, all of us in Michael's path are nursing gaping wounds left when the businesses, homes, or even the existence we had accepted as "normal" were torn away from us. With so many patients and no doctors or even an operating room available, the wounds begin to fester and seethe with infection. Everyone begins pointing fingers at their best hope for an ally.

"The new normal" is a phrase both beach and town peeps are united in matriculating into our social verbiage. It translates as our weary community's collective wry sigh; the dim acknowledgement that the landmarks and signals our brains frantically search for to validate every truth we've ever known, will be scrambled forever. The structure we've so diligently programmed into daily life through decades of public schooling and casual Fridays and right-turns at the Burger King is now nothing more than a garbage-strewn debris pile we're left to bewilderedly sort through.

"Hurry; this buy-one-get-one-free tanning membership is available for a limited time only," the sexy radio girl spouts as we drive through the movie set style destruction. My kids and I crack up at the ridiculousness of it. Imagine! Tanning? Who could be thinking of such frivolity?

My older son *tsk-tsks* arrogantly at the wasted advertising dollars, my daughter wonders whether the tanning place is actually still standing. We all revel at the chance to laugh, grateful at the relief; marveling at the source. Will tanning beds and other such nonsense be considered "normal" again someday?

Part of me hopes so. Part of me struggles to hope at all, at times.

But just like Michael, I believe it will pass.

~

I think I'm slipping.
Falling back into a place
I don't want to be

— *Jason Hedden*

~

#LifeafterMichael

WHEN THERE WAS NO ELECTRICITY
PAULETTE PERLMAN

~

("Me cooking hot water on a camp stove to clean dishes in my underwear.")

Is anyone there?
There must be someone who cares —
Not just the black bear

— Donna Williams

~

I'M SORRY THEY'VE FORGOTTEN
JESSICA ST. HILL

I'm sorry they've forgotten you,
In the chase for bleeding ledes.
The images of fallen forests,
Your basic human needs.
The cameras now are all packed up,
They've slammed the news vans' doors.
I'm sorry that your suffering isn't "sexy" anymore.

The posts I see of tiny progress
Managed here and there,
Make me weep and turn away,
Because it hurts to care.
It hurts far more to live it though,
So I keep your pain alive,
Sharing till my fingers ache,
Your spirit that's survived.

Downtown streets are looking great,
The power is on again.
But too many homes are only filled
With whispers of absent friends.
"She moved away." "They left this week."
Is now the sad refrain
Of a city ringed with broken wood,
Of a township laced with pain.

I miss you. You are my hearttown.

You were where I gained my voice.
The place I learned to live again
When life left little choice.
The house I lived in, crushed and gone,
By trees I'd held so dear.
But I'll never forget the love I found,
And friends I've cherished here.

~

MEN DON'T CRY
TONY SIMMONS

At the fringe of the Pythagorean Forest, where pines bowed to the south, beaten down and never to rise again, a man stood with plastic bucket in hand.

Rubber waders and denim shorts. Torso glistening with days of unwashed sweat. Sharp pine acids in his nose. Brown water up to his ankles.

The survivor listened. Sounds drifted on slow, humid gusts. Occasional shouts. Gurgle of tannin mud under his shifting weight. Insect buzz of distant chainsaws. Crack of hard wood splitting under assault, the trees dying as slowly as they'd aged. Broken by ancient powers and dissected by amateurs.

Equidistant to infinity came the persistent thump-thump-thump of helicopters on patrol, passing beyond a horizon stripped bare to blue sky. And somewhere, sirens sang Doppler Effect tests. He could see so much farther today, yet the sirens remained invisible because he could hear so much farther still.

No birds sang. No squirrels scampered. Sometimes a dog's bark would break the quiet. But the electric background noise of life had fled. Gone were the indefinable communal sounds of a neighborhood's air handlers, of traffic on a distant street, of music playing too loud in a house too nearby.

The day was paper, bright and silent, with nothing to write upon it and no one willing to read.

Bucket by bucket, he filled plastic totes on the back porch, storing dark water to refill the tanks of toilets in the house without shingles or light, where ceilings sagged and threatened to fall like the sky had done already.

At night, lying awake on perspiration-damp sheets, hearing the grumble of generators at other houses. Random reports of gunfire like popping champagne corks. Wondering about tomorrow.

Wind noise moaned through shattered eaves, and his heart raced, tripping, like it did when his ears popped and the windows blew out and the yard disappeared behind a white wall of rain and debris. Wind so hard it air shattered.

A text from someone he couldn't save was the last thing his phone gave up before the aether died.

He carries the blame like buckets of seepage, uses it to flush his fear and loathing. He lies under its weight at night, unable to breathe, wishing he could drown. He stands beneath the firmament of so many unfamiliar stars, feeling insignificant, talking to the invisible and considering the unthinkable.

Anger takes its toll, and men don't cry.

Except, sometimes. In the dark, when water drains from his eyes and dries on his face, when breath is so brittle it cracks.

Storms can't see you in the dark, and they'll never know. And even if they suspect, tears and sweat taste much the same.

That's the best time.

~

ABOUT THE PROJECT

We asked for your poems, your essays, your short stories, your art and photographs created in the wake and wreckage of Hurricane Michael. We wanted to hear from you, the Hurricane Michael survivors. We wanted to publish your work in a compendium which would be used to raise funds for a local relief charity.

While it was still open and raw. Before we got distance or perspective. As we climbed out of the darkness. We encouraged fellow victims to speak, write, draw, paint, sculpt, photograph. What this world-changing, life-changing event meant in the now. To you. To your loved ones and friends.

We were only just walking out of the wilderness together. And we hoped to see what it means.

Work chosen from the submissions was included at the sole discretion of the editor. There was no limit to style, subject or length. But there was a deadline: midnight on Nov. 9, 2018, as we wanted to publish while the wound remained red and raw, as soon as possible, before the grief faded or the second thoughts began to surface.

The hope was to tell our story together, and help make a difference in the aftermath.

We hope we succeeded. Regardless, we hope you will all take care of each other out there.

If we've learned anything through this, it's that we're all we have.

Tony Simmons
Panama City Beach
November 2018

CPSIA information can be obtained
at www.ICGtesting.com
Printed in the USA
LVHW032145221118
597954LV00002B/687/P